God's Love Story:

The Tower of Babel
Book 6

By R. Lane Lender

STORIES OF LIFE PRODUCTIONS

God's Love Story: The Tower of Babel, Book 6

Copyright © 2020 By Stories of Life Productions

ISBN: 978-1-970032-11-6 (Hard Cover)

ISBN: 978-1-970032-12-3 (eBook)

For more information about Stories of Life Productions and/or God's Love Story Visual Bible visit www.glsvb.org.

All rights reserved. No part of this publication may be reproduced, stored in a retrieval system, or transmitted in any form or by any means – electronic, mechanical, photocopy, recording, or any other – except for brief quotations in printed reviews, without the prior permission of Stories of Life Productions.

Published in the United States of America

Introduction

God's Love Story Children's Book Series is dedicated to my grandchildren. One of the greatest gifts a parent can pass off to their children is a passion to love Jesus more than anything else in this world. This passion is more caught than taught. Our children need to see our love for Jesus and they too will follow in our footsteps. My wife and I are truly blessed to not only have godly parents but to have two wonderful children, now in their mid twenties, who have learned to love Jesus from birth. As I write, my son is a prosecuting attorney in Texas and my daughter is married to a wonderful man, a dedicated Christ follower. They now have one child and their hope is many more. My daughter is also preparing to homeschool them all like she and her brother were. My desire is to provide a biblically-based tool for parents to use to cultivate in their children a love for Jesus in their most precious and formative years. I desire nothing more than to see my future grandchildren come to know Jesus and to develop into solid Kingdom contributing Christ followers. Thus, I submit this contribution. My prayer is that this book series develops in your children a love for the gospel and a passion for Jesus.

I also want to thank you for your purchase of this book and the other books in this series (See the back cover for more details). Your purchase goes directly to support Stories of Life Productions as we continue to produce, promote, and distribute God's Love Story Visual Bible (GLSVB). GLSVB is an oral story Bible created for the cell phone that has been translated into several languages of Unreached People Groups (UPGs). These UPGs live in places that are very difficult to access with the gospel. Because of your purchase, as well as gifts from generous donors, GLSVB is provided free to missionaries and believers around the world who are using this tool for evangelism and discipleship. GLSVB can be accessed at www.hikayaat.com. To find out more information, order books, or help us promote God's Love Story Children's Book series or GLSVB, visit www.glsvb.org. May God's Love Story Children's Books give you and your child a passion to serve Christ and His Kingdom's purpose!

Sincerely,
R. Lane Lender
Stories of Life Productions
contact@glsvb.org
www.hikayaat.com
www.glsvb.org

After the flood the descendants of Noah,
Multiplied with many a birth;
Wrapped up in pride, one language worldwide,
They failed to spread through the earth;

As one people, they migrated South,
And East to the plane of Shinar;
With heart and soul, a great city their goal,
Built of mud bricks and tar;

They said to each other, "Let's build a great tower,
That reaches high in the sky";
Ignoring God's plan to fill the earth,
Rebellious they would not comply;

God saw their pride and rebellious nature,
There was nothing they could not do;
One tongue, one nation was trouble in the makin',
No limit to sin, pee-u!

God said "Let's go down and confuse their language,
So they cannot understand";
Construction was halted, their plan altered,
Their scheme of rebellion disband;

As you may have noticed, even the flood,
Did not change mankind's nature;
Continuing in pride and rebelliousness,
Depravity grew greater and greater;

The Bible says clearly that mankind's nature,
Is corrupted through and through;
Dead in your sins and your trespasses,
There's only one thing you can do;

Give your life to Jesus, surrender your all,
Forgiveness in Him you will find;
He died for my sins and for your sins too,
Sin's penalty He wants to unwind;

He died on the cross to give you new life,
The lamb of great sacrifice;
God's wrath satisfied, let go of your pride,
His substitution will suffice;

The proof of His victory over our sin,
Is found in His resurrection;
On the 3rd day according to Scripture,
He arose to seal our election;

So swallow your pride, surrender to God,
Don't be like the ones in this story;
Give Jesus your heart, you'll find a new start,
And give to God all the glory!

Lightning Source UK Ltd.
Milton Keynes UK
UKHW050251010920
369114UK00004B/132